SANTA FE
AND NORTHERN NEW MEXICO

BY JACK PARSONS

INTRODUCTION BY CHRISTINE MATHER
DESIGN BY PAUL HARDY

RIZZOLI
NEW YORK

For Becky, Chris,
and Alex, with love

ACKNOWLEDGMENTS

Many people helped contribute to
this book, but I owe a special debt of
gratitude to a few whose support and
generous spirit over the long haul or
in the brief period of publication
proved invaluable: Michael Earney,
Bill Clark, Barry and Nicki Abrams,
Marie Romero Cash, Bill Field, Mac
and Marjorie Parsons, Jack Loeffler,
Karen Hyatt and Siegfried Halus.
Thanks also to Christine Mather, my
good friend, who was kind enough to
write the Introduction with her usual
skill and understanding, to Paul
Hardy who brought his marvellous
eye to the design of this book, and to
Lois Brown, under whose able guid-
ance the book took shape.

First published in 1991 in the United States of
America by Rizzoli International Publications, Inc.
300 Park Avenue South, New York, New York
10010

Copyright © 1991 by Rizzoli International
Publications, Inc.
Illustrations copyright © Jack Parsons

Library of Congress Cataloging-in-Publication
Data

Parsons, Jack, 1939-
Santa Fe and Northern New Mexico/Jack
Parsons; introduction by Christine Mather.
p.   cm.
ISBN 0-8478-1333-9
1. Santa Fe Region (N.M.)—Description and
travel—Views. 2. New Mexico—Description
and travel—1981- —Views. I. Title.
F804.S243P37 1991   90-50797
978.9'56—dc20   CIP

Map by Lundquist Design, New York

Printed and bound in Japan

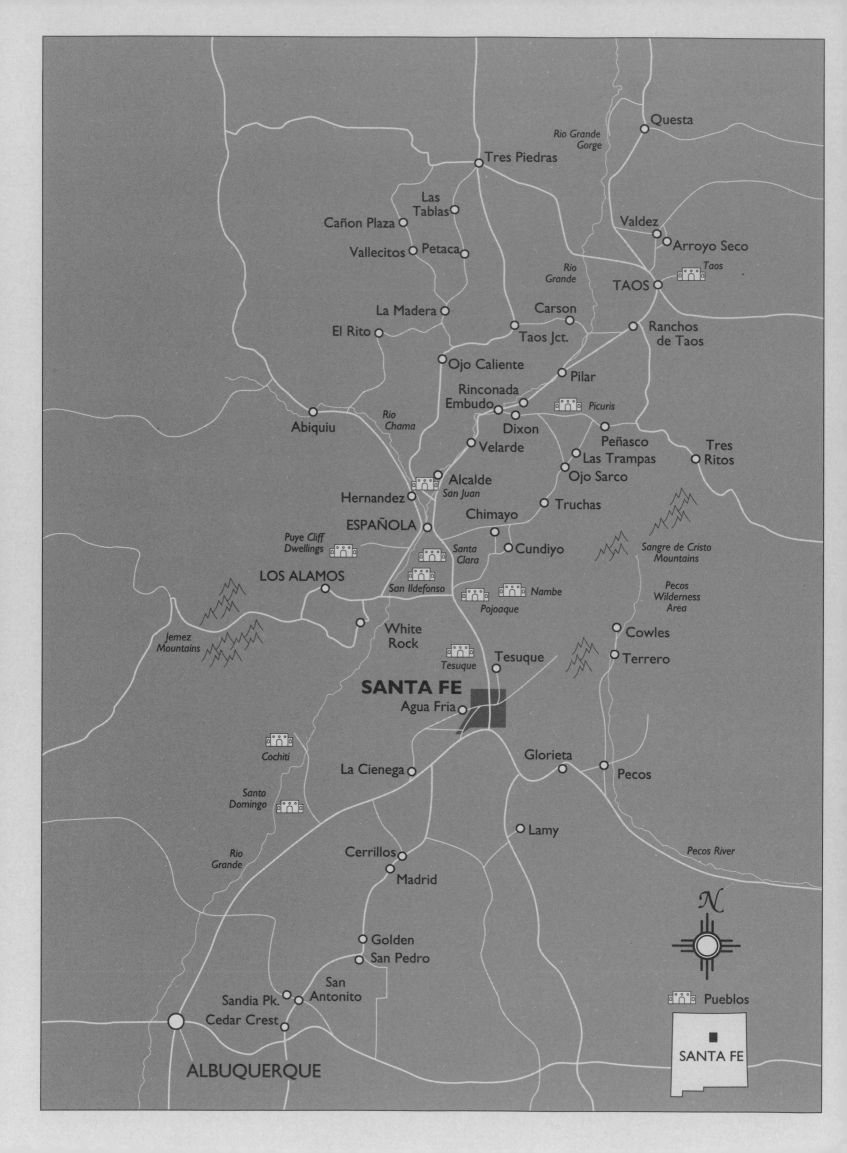

INTRODUCTION

Over the centuries thousands have submitted happily to the lure of New Mexico and its fountainhead, Santa Fe. To abandon oneself to the profound natural beauty of the land is to allow the senses to dominate body and soul, for New Mexico is, above all, a physical experience that touches the senses and floods the mind with powerful associations. This is a place where one experiences heightened awareness, a fact not lost on many.

The palpable nature of New Mexico can be daunting; it can force mental and physical upheaval in a life—more than a few casual visits to New Mexico have turned into an abandonment of a former life or a perpetual cycle of repeat visits. For those who live in Santa Fe, it is always a joy to return after travel; there is a distinct feeling of well-being that comes from climbing La Bajada and viewing the mountains spread out before you like a gift. In this unparalleled landscape it is quite possible and, in fact, reasonable to accept and be happy with one's place in nature.

Nowhere is the directness and power of New Mexico more apparent than in the many aspects of the landscape. It is an immoderate place given to wild shows of raw beauty brought on by a turbulent geologic past everywhere in evidence. Mountains thrust and heave, while yesterday's lava stands nearby; giant calderas and barely extinct volcanos let us know with a daily presence that human life on the planet is a mere wink. The landscape seems barely softened by more recent geological events. Trees, bushes, and grasses fight the long, hard New Mexican battle against the eternal lack of sufficient moisture. It is hard to believe that scrawny bands of chickenlike dinosaurs—Coelophysis, our state fossil—and their giant relatives once devoured one another and fed on lush vegetation at the shores of an inland sea. Textbook stratigraphy abounds with ribbons of geologic time laid out in layers of delicate color. It is clear that much time and life have passed by here.

The power of nature and humanity's place within the natural world are the primary themes suggested by this striking region; they are themes which have been a focus of life for many millennia. The narrow threads of water that cut through the lands of the Southwest, coming from the high timbered areas and flowing through and yielding to mesa and desert, define human life in the region. Along these waters live the Pueblo people. Here are the traditional homelands, so ancient that their histories are lost to recorded time but are the subject of mystery and timeless belief. Nowhere in our land is the history of man and place so inextricably united—the people of the Pueblos define this place; New Mexico without them is unimaginable. Their life upon this land represents the longest and the most continuous record of human habitation in our country. From this continuity comes great diversity, compelling architecture and lifestyle, some of the greatest pottery and basketry traditions known, and a profound lesson concerning our place within nature. All of these fruits of longevity upon the land were hard won.

Prehistory stretches back to the time of the hunters and gatherers with their refined and elegant stone implements. Early sites of human presence are represented by such implements and a few modest holes indicating the basic structure of the dwellings. The great leap forward toward a Pueblo civilization of complexity and diversity came with the advent of cultigens—a technology that gradually entered the Southwest from Mesoamerica. Even before the glimmer of the Christian era had arrived in the Old World, in the northern backwater of the great civilizations be-

---

Wagon camp in front of T. Corrick Livery Stable, 104 Don Gaspar Avenue, Santa Fe, about 1915. *Photograph by T. Harmon Parkhurst, courtesy Museum of New Mexico.*

ing formed in Central America, the famed Indian triad of beans, squash, and corn had brought to the people of the Southwest a new way of life. Hunting and gathering remained an important adjunct to the vagaries of agriculture, but with agriculture came the opportunity for large, settled populations. Those populations that came to dwell over the centuries in the many diverse areas of Northern New Mexico, as well as parts of Arizona and Southern Colorado, are the ancestors of the present-day Pueblo people—they are the Anasazi.

The legacy of the Anasazi is thrilling. To those who love the Southwest, this exotic name conjures up a sense of profound mystery, spirituality, serenity, and beauty. Canyon de Chelly, Chaco Canyon, and Mesa Verde are America's premier archeological sites, not only because of the compelling locations in which each is set or because of the architectural remains and objects but rather because they are places of transcendent beauty—rare spots where man, nature, and spirituality are perfectly balanced.

Of the broad Southwestern area occupied by the Anasazi, with a date of cultural continuity beginning around the first century A.D., those defined as the Eastern Anasazi inhabited the area of Northern New Mexico and served as the ancestors of the contemporary Rio Grande Pueblos as well as Acoma and Laguna Pueblos. Along the Rio Grande and its main tributaries live the people of the Pueblos, in Taos, Picuris, San Juan,

Santa Clara, San Ildefonso, Nambe, Pojoaque, Tesuque, Sandia, Isleta, Cochiti, Santo Domingo, San Felipe, Santa Ana, Zia, Jemez, while to the west live the other Pueblo peoples and their cultural relatives, such as the Acoma, Laguna, Zuni, and Hopi groups. Together they share a common history of time spent in the great Southwest. This common history and shared lifestyle gives to the entire region an underlying unity that stretches back over thousands of years and continues to serve as the basis of identity both for the Pueblo people and for many of those who have followed.

Despite this unity there is also a baffling amount of diversity among historic and contemporary groups of Pueblo people. While the Pueblos are often regarded as being the same, they are in fact often quite different. Various distinctive language groups such as Keres, Tewa, and Towa are clear markers to linguists of divergent backgrounds as are distinctive patterns of kinship and social organization. Ritual and ceremonial life take on a variety of forms as well, but the underlying unity of the region is confirmed by the fact that ritual life throughout the area focuses on the continual need for rain, with its promise of renewal and life, and upon the ongoing need for balance and harmony within the community. These two basic aspects of life in the Southwest are asserted over and over again in a ritual context and find visual form in the arts and functional crafts that were developed in support of these basic human needs. Every aspect of life—from the dance on the plaza, to the kachina doll given to the child, to the painted pattern on the pot, to the greeting to a friend, to the seed placed in the ground—contains the essence of these beliefs. While these fundamentals of unity are continually asserted, so too is the immense complexity of the Pueblo people and their societies. For example, among the Zunis there are twelve clans and thirteen medicine societies. In addition, all males are members of a mask dance society. Each tribal member must also contend with the demands of Western religious groups, secular local government, and the national government. The complexity of these religious and social patterns is only partially known and understood by those outside the soci-

Taos Pueblo in 1878. *Photograph by B. H. Gurnsey, courtesy Museum of New Mexico.*

ety since much ritual and belief are private, secret, and sacred. What is seen by the outsider today comes in the form of dance, music, and ritual that is presented for all people as part of ancient rituals of renewal and well-being. The ancient functional crafts of the past that carry the markers of their spiritual context in the continuance of time-worn designs today are often purchased and appreciated by visitors to the Southwest as examples of fine American craft.

The contribution of the Pueblos to American culture comes not only in the form of crafts available to the public but also as a legacy of pride for many other Native American groups. As settled agriculturalists living on ancient tribal lands and as direct descendants of the Anasazi, the Pueblo people have served as a refuge and resource of Native American values. Conservative traditionalists, such as those dwelling at Taos Pueblo, have eschewed such commonplace modern amenities as electricity and have led successful legal battles to recapture important spiritual sites such as Blue Lake. This emphasis on assertion of tribal rights and sovereignty in order to combat the forces of acculturation comes from hard-won experience gained over hundreds of years of contact with the non-native world.

The initial thrust of the Spanish into the New World was marked by a desire to gain wealth, particularly mineral wealth, and to extend the reach of Spanish domination. Following early, inaccurate reports of wealth to be found to the north, Francisco Vásquez de Coronado set out from central Mexico in 1540 for the northern reaches. Impelled by the quest for cities of gold, Coronado left a trail of brutality and terror that gave the inhabitants of the region a dreadful preview of what was to come. Subsequent Spanish visitations to the region were met initially with attempts by the natives to greet the outsiders in a peaceful manner, but increasing demands from the Spanish for goods and control sparked rebellion. The Spanish felt compelled to make examples of those who would not submit to their demands and forced oppression soon followed. There were starts and stops to the intrusion of the Spanish into the region from the time of the Coronado expedition until the entrance of Juan de

San Francisco Street, Santa Fe, about 1897-98. *Photograph by John B. Reall, courtesy Museum of New Mexico.*

Oñate to the Rio Grande valley in 1598. The hope for mineral wealth, the desire for further colonization, and the need to extend Christianity into the region, brought Oñate and his soldiers, colonists, and friars northward. Precious metals were not to be found, causing the Spanish under Oñate to exact support from the native populations by forcing them to give up limited supplies of corn and other food as well as commandeering labor and supplies of woven goods from the Pueblos. Those who rebelled were enslaved or killed. This insupportable pattern continued for eighty years.

Thoughts by the Spanish of abandoning the region due to its poverty gave way to an urgency to Christianize this large, unsettled population. In areas that even today remain remote, Spanish missions were constructed to carry on the program of Christian education. In the Salinas Basin the missions of Quarai, Abo, and Gran Quivira are monumental reminders of the immensity of the drive and ambition to carry forth religion into the wilderness. The large populations that once built these classic structures are now gone but the edifices remain as enormous documents of the meeting of cultures. The pattern of missionizing, colonizing, and exacting tribute was devastating not only to the morale of the native populations but to their numbers as well—it was a pattern that eventually became intolerable. Attempts on the part of the Pueblos to compromise or meet Spanish demands had been continually thwarted both by corruption within Spanish government and by

conflict between the secular government and the mission authorities.

Despite the differences, particularly of language, among the Pueblo groups, plans were gradually evolved to expel the Spanish from their domain. A well-thought-out plan involving war chiefs and leaders from most of the Pueblos was put into action on August 10, 1680, and led to what is widely regarded as the single most effective action taken by Native Americans in the New World against outside authority. All of the Spanish were expelled from Northern New Mexico and a significant number were killed. All evidence of Spanish occupation was then systematically destroyed, especially objects of religious significance. The Pueblo Revolt of 1680 thus brought to an end, though briefly, the oppression of Spanish rule to the north. By 1692 the Spanish were back, this time under the leadership of Don Diego de Vargas. They had returned to stay.

The decades following the revolt and during the reconquest were especially trying times for the Pueblo people. Serious erosion of the populations, dislocations of people, intertribal factionalism, and other social disruptions took a heavy toll on native groups throughout New Mexico. Fortunately, the previous fourscore years of Spanish heavy-handedness were to be moderated; the government became more responsive and less exacting, while the efforts of the missionaries were also softened. But the real coming together of Spanish and Pueblos was the result of another factor—the joining of forces against a common foe. By the eighteenth century the effectiveness of marauding nomadic groups—Apache, Navajo, Ute, and Comanche—brought about an alliance between Spanish and Pueblo for a shared defense.

Though these nomadic groups came to the Southwest much later than the Pueblo people, they nonetheless had great impact on the region. The Navajo, especially during the nineteenth century, began to make serious forays into Northern New Mexico. Fear of the Navajo as raiders was tempered by a great respect for their abilities, especially as weavers and later as silversmiths. Borrowing from the Pueblos by the Navajos, in part through their adoption of aspects of religious belief and weaving techniques, is well

substantiated. But while the Navajos borrowed the method of weaving from the Pueblos and the means from the Spanish (in the form of wool introduced to the New World), the final products displayed features that were distinctly Navajo and remain a significant contribution to the arts of the New World.

Eventually dreams of conquest and immense wealth were moderated and the Spanish settled into Northern New Mexico as farmers, laboring under the same harsh conditions as their Pueblo neighbors. New Mexico became a true backwater of the mighty Spanish Empire. Mostly forgotten, often ignored, the butt of the central authorities and the dread of the colonial administrator—New Mexico seemed to have nothing worthy of exploiting. Services and supplies were grudgingly sent from central Mexico to aid both church and state in the region. The colonists did survive, however, and if they did not prosper, they became resilient and toughened in response to their environment. All the while, the underlying strength of the region was continually reasserted as Santa Fe was located at the axis of the meeting of two important cultures—Latin and Anglo American. The little Plaza was the terminus of two great pathways, the Camino Real and the Santa Fe Trail. Mule trains made the long journey north to the Plaza at Santa Fe and disgorged their products of Mexico proper—tools, candles, fancy cloth, weapons, paper, and books—and took back with them the modest products of the fron-

"Famous Team of Trotters." Burro wagon at the Plaza, Santa Fe, 1912. *Photograph by Jesse L. Nusbaum, courtesy Museum of New Mexico.*

tier—woven wool and cotton, and pinyon nuts. By the beginning of the nineteenth century, the Spanish Empire had became a moldering relic of earlier, headier times. For those in New Mexico their isolation had left them with little loyalty to Spain so that when Mexico declared independence from Spain in 1821, they went along with the change, while keeping their own counsel.

New Mexicans had become a folk unto themselves. They were equally wary of Spanish administrators, Mexican bureaucrats, and Yankee traders. Known to be polite but intractable, New Mexicans had quite literally become New Mexicans, and they regarded all those from outside as outsiders. They were immune to criticism and were intent on doing things in their own manner and in their own sweet time. The declared independence from Spain would now allow New Mexico to be opened up for trade on the Santa Fe Trail. New Mexico's potential as a link to commerce with Mexico had long been recognized by merchants and traders eager to penetrate its borders. In their typical free-wheeling manner, New Mexicans were happy to do business with all and Santa Fe quickly became the hub of this activity. The Mexicans, however, were not so pleased with the assertive young American traders who quickly established business ties in Santa Fe. Their concern was well founded, for the territorial ambitions of the young American nation

"The Old Carreda." Laguna Pueblo, 1880s. *Photograph by W. H. Jackson & Co., courtesy the Henry E. Huntington Library.*

were on the rise; the Pacific beckoned and New Mexico was but one spot along this route. New Mexico was to be a part of the dream of one nation from coast to coast, and the Mexicans were to be the losers.

The first Americans to visit Santa Fe seemed to have been uniformly shocked by what they saw. Accustomed to a world of mortar, brick, and frame, American visitors from the East during the nineteenth century could not fathom the architecture of the town. The simple low-lying homes of adobe were merely mud to them, just the soft earth against the bright sky. There were exceptions. Young Susan Magoffin's diary of her journey into New Mexico and Mexico in 1846–1847 is a remarkable piece of observation for that time. At age eighteen, not only was she the first American woman to enter Santa Fe, she just happened to be along when the American Army, under Stephan Watts Kearny, claimed New Mexico. Leaving the Plains behind, she first saw the mountains of Northern New Mexico, "From the greatest hight (sic) to which I have yet ascended on horse-back, mountains far more lofty than any I've seen, deep vallies (sic) below that looked blue so great was the distance to them; the clouds seemed resting on the mountains around us. Oh, for the genius of an artist that I might pencil such scenes otherwise than in my memory . . . that I might trace with this pen a more lively and correct sketch of some of nature's grandest and most striking works."

While Susan Magoffin may have lacked the ability to adequately describe the magical new world that was being opened up to America, she was to be followed by others who would eloquently capture with pen and brush the enchanting beauty they were to discover. Others were unimpressed by the dry landscape and harsh living conditions, but gambled that American ingenuity would somehow be able to transform this apparent wasteland into a productive region, as had happened in every other territory gained along the road of westward expansion. But New Mexico would yield its riches and charms only to those with the patience and perception to stay for the long haul and for the love of the land.

Santa Fe cannot easily be compared to any other place and to do so would be an injustice.

B 3007. Old San Miguel Church, Santa Fe, N. M.

"Old San Miguel Church, Santa Fe, New Mexico," 1880.

Just as New Mexicans had become a distinct breed, so too had their homeland become a distinct experience. Influx of diverse populations and then isolation of the region had brought together separate cultures in a unique blending and an uneasy harmony. The Americans were to add to this mix. Those who influenced the area most were precisely the ones who had the greatest appreciation of its qualities.

As early as 1910, some of the new residents were already worried that Santa Fe was in danger of becoming yet another Anytown, U.S.A. The first to recognize the danger and to take action to stem the tide of homogenization were members of a growing art colony; artists drawn to the exotic nature of the cultures, fascinated by the vernacular architecture, and enthralled with the brilliance of the landscape and light. Along with the community of anthropologists in the area, they rushed to record traditional ways of Native and Hispanic life. They led the preservation struggle to salvage dying adobe monuments and to build new ones in the traditional fashion. But the primary contribution that this influential group of artists and anthropologists made was to fall deeply and completely in love with life in New Mexico. For some, living and creating in New Mexico would represent the best years of their lives; for others, it became their lives. Many stayed on to discover and rediscover the beauty of place. Their memories were of nights sleeping under the stars on the way to Taos with the axle broken, of being frozen at dawn while watching the Deer dancers emerge from the morning light on the hills at San Ildefonso, of standing on the roof of the car with the camera waiting for the moon to rise over Hernandez, and of digging, digging, digging at Pecos, Quarai, Gran Quivira, Frijoles Canyon, under the Palace, or in the Archives of the Indies for the find of a lifetime, of lugging the hundreth oversized adobe brick only to watch the wall melt away in the spring.

Many seasons have passed since Ansel Adams caught the moon and Elsie Parsons the words to an ancient song, and since the wall melted on the Camino at Will Shuster's house, and the morning glories bloomed at Georgia O'Keeffe's door. When the fall season comes, the red chiles are hung by the thousands in Velarde and the bright red against the sky makes the heavens bluer. At Taos Pueblo, how many centuries has it been since the pole has gone up and been greased for the climbing competition? When the winter snow comes, the evening air along Acequia Madre fills with the distinct odor of burning pinyon pine; soon Christmas will arrive and with it the farolitos. Will the wind and the sleet ever stop in the spring; perhaps, when the lilacs bloom and the Castilian roses come forth. How did the Spanish colonists ever survive, one asks oneself in July, while cleaning up the remains of a garden covered with six inches of hail.

New Mexico definitely has its distinct seasons, each passing without regard to human activities. Perhaps because the sky is so big, the air is so dry, and the seasons so strong, the human cycles are carefully defined. For the Native Americans, the solstice and anticipated rain are life-defining factors; while for the Hispanics, the Catholic calendar, with its saint days and ancient Christian celebrations, delineates the passage of time and the changing of the seasons. The Anglo Americans try to fit into the schedules of the Native Americans and Hispanics, but often with misguided zeal and the inevitable commercialism, missing the point of the quiet, repetitive human act. The fiestas and dances and feast days and saint days that fill the ritual calendars of ancient religions are the markers of time—of lives passing. We live in hope that though Santa Fe will change, the magic somehow will remain.

But for a *greatness* of beauty I have never experienced anything like New Mexico. All those mornings when I went with a hoe along the ditch to the Cañon, at the ranch, and stood, in the fierce, proud silence of the Rockies, on their foothills, to look far over the desert to the blue mountains away in Arizona, blue as chalcedony, with the sage-brush desert sweeping grey-blue in between, dotted with tiny cube-crystals of houses, the vast amphitheatre of lofty, indomitable desert, sweeping round to the ponderous Sangre de Cristo, mountains on the east, and coming up flush at the pine-dotted foot-hills of the Rockies! What splendour! Only the tawny eagle could really sail out into the splendour of it all. Leo Stein once wrote to me: It is the most aesthetically-satisfying landscape I know. To me it was much more than that. It had a splendid silent terror, and a vast far-and-wide magnificence which made it way beyond mere aesthetic appreciation. Never is the light more pure and overweening than there, arching with a royalty almost cruel over the hollow, uptilted world. For it is curious that the land which has produced modern political democracy at its highest pitch should give one the greatest sense of overweening, terrible proudness and mercilessness: but so beautiful, God! so beautiful! Those that have spent morning after morning alone there pitched among the pines above the great proud world of desert will know, almost unbearably how beautiful it is, how clear and unquestioned is the might of the day. Just day itself is tremendous there.
                                                                —D. H. Lawrence

Eaves Ranch, Santa Fe

Santa Fe

Inn at Loretto, Santa Fe

Camino del Monte Sol, Santa Fe

Canyon Road, Santa Fe

Don Gaspar Avenue, Santa Fe

Villanueva

Santa Fe

Santa Fe

La Cienega

Santa Fe

East DeVargas Street, Santa Fe

El Rancho de las Golondrinas, La Cienega

Taos

さくら

Sakura
Sushi Bar
JAPANESE CUISINE

San Francisco Street, Santa Fe

Don Gaspar Avenue, Santa Fe

Chile Ristras, Santa Fe

Chiles, Alcalde

Santa Fe

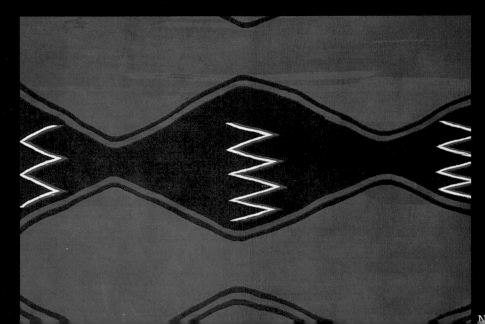

Navajo Germantown blanket

Canyon Road, Santa Fe

El Rey Inn, Santa Fe

Plaza, Santa Fe

Canyon Road, Santa Fe

Santa Fe

La Fonda Hotel, Santa Fe

Santa Fe

Santa Fe

El Rancho de las Golondrinas, La Cienega

Pecos National Monument

Taos Pueblo

Hornos, El Rancho de las Golondrinas, La Cienega

Los Miradores, Santa Fe

Santa Fe

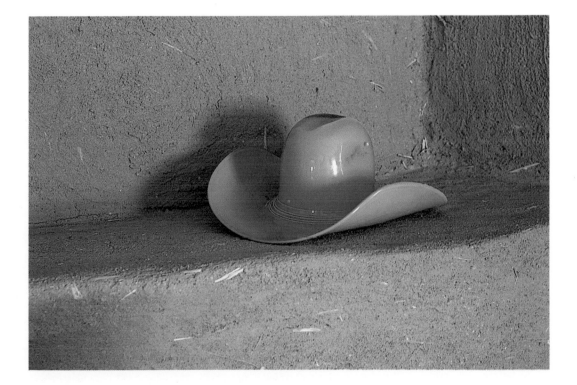

Cerro Gordo Road, Santa Fe

José Archuleta, violin, and Ramón Archuleta, guitar, Los Matachines de Arroyo Seco, Taos

Leandro Tórrez and Cruz Romero, Las Vegas

Violinista, El Rancho de las Golondrinas, La Cienega

Rafael Lobato, El Rancho de las Golondrinas, La Cienega

Emilio Romero, tinworker, Spanish Market, Santa Fe

Maria Vergara-Wilson, weaver, Ojo Caliente

Carding wool, El Rancho de las Golondrinas, La Cienega

Penasco Valley and Sangre de Cristo Mountains

South of Costilla

Eaves Ranch movie set, Santa Fe

Truchas

Costilla

Cordova

San Acacia Church, Rodarte

Chevy pickup, La Cienega

Valle Grande, Jemez Mountains

Abiquiu

Villanueva

Cabin, Pecos Wilderness

El Rancho de las Golondrinas, La Cienega

Madrid

Abiquiu

Tent Rocks, Cochití

Abiquiu

Abiquiu

El Vado Lake

Heron Lake

San Miguel del Vado, Ribera

San Isidro, Santa Cruz

San Juan Nepomuceno, Llano de San Juan

San José y Niño

Altar, Santuario de Chimayó, Chimayó

Tin frame with print

Detail, punched tin nicho

San Miguel, Marie Romero Cash

Nuestra Señora de Guadalupe, Marie Romero Cash

San José de Gracia, Las Trampas

Sagrada Familia, Rowe

San Geronimo de Taos, Taos Pueblo

Cross of the Martyrs, Santa Fe

San José de Gracia, Las Trampas

Abiquiu

Santa Rita, Lucero

Santa Fe

Chama River

Taos

El Rancho de las Golondrinas, La Cienega

Sangre de Cristo Mountains, Santa Fe

Sangre de Cristo Mountains, Santa Fe

El Rancho de las Golondrinas, La Cienega

Bosque del Apache Wildlife Refuge

Abiquiu

Taos Gorge

Chimayó

Arroyo Seco, Taos

El Rancho de las Golondrinas, La Cienega

Vallecitos

San Juan Pueblo

Velarde

Los Ojos

Chama River north of Abiquiu

Abiquiu

South of Galisteo

Sand Hill Cranes

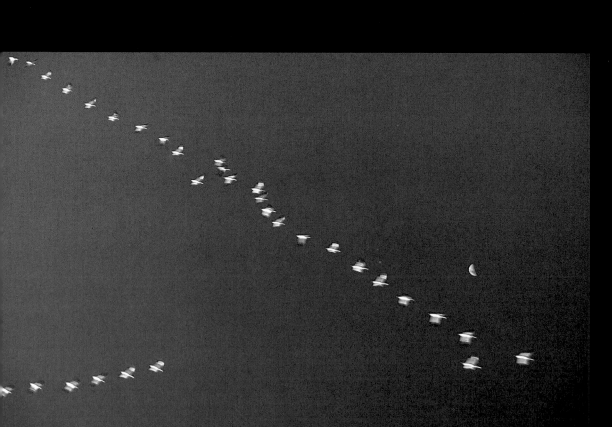

Sand Hill Cranes

FESTIVALS AND FEAST DAYS

Festivals, feast days, dances, and Native American and Spanish markets abound all year in Santa Fe, in the small towns and villages, and at the Pueblos. The traditional festivals commemorate the patron saint of the town or a historical event. But there are also art, crafts, music, and film festivals. The most elaborate of these takes place during September in Santa Fe. A giant 40-foot-tall puppet called Zozobra is torched, opening a two-day fiesta celebrating the city's cultural traditions.

Each Pueblo has its own annual feast day, with plentiful food and colorful dances. The purpose of this day is to give thanks for the health and well-being of the community. Feast day at the Pueblos goes back for centuries, well before the Spanish came to New Mexico. When the Spanish priests became aware of these festivities, they named each feast day for a saint on whose day the feast was held.

Dancing is an important part of this centuries-old tradition, and dances such as the Corn, Buffalo, Butterfly, Basket, Deer, and Elk are a renewal of the Pueblo people's bond to earth, sky, the spirits, and the animals, whom they consider their brothers. These events are solemn as well as playful, and clowns, representing discontinuity and irony in the world, often are part of the religious ceremony.

Feast days primarily are for residents and friends; it is a time to give thanks and renew old friendships. The people of the Pueblos, however, invite visitors to share these ancient rituals and to taste the traditional foods and view the crafts.

SANTA FE FESTIVALS

FEBRUARY

Winterfestival: For skiers, includes races, snow sculpture competitions, music, and food. Information: (505) 983-5615

MAY

Santa Fe Festival of the Arts: Runs for 10 days at the end of May. Includes exhibits, lectures, music, dance, and theater. Information: (505) 988-3924 or write to 1524 Paseo de Peralta, Santa Fe, NM 87501

JULY

Traditional Spanish Market: Last full weekend of July. Exhibits of embroidery, textiles, weaving, straw, tinwork, jewelry, and furniture. Information: write to Spanish Colonial Arts Society, P.O. Box 1611, Santa Fe, NM 87501

Rodeo de Santa Fe: Includes saddle broncos, Brahma bulls, calf roping, and steer wrestling. Information: (505) 982-4659

AUGUST

Indian Market: A juried competition including handmade baskets, pottery, rugs, jewelry, drums, etc. All genuine Indian handicrafts. Information: (505) 983-5220 or write to South Western Association on Indian Affairs (S.W.A.I.A.), P.O. Box 1964, Santa Fe, NM 87501

Banjo and Fiddle Minifestival: Runs for two days. Competitions of banjo, fiddle, guitar, mandolin, and bluegrass. Information: (505) 983-8315 or 982-9548, or write to Route 7, Box 115-BK, Santa Fe, NM 87505

Rainbow Warrior Music and Arts Festival: One-day event held in Paolo Soleri Amphitheater features singers, dancers, and storytellers. Proceeds go to the Tides Foundation, which supports the artistic and spiritual traditions of indigenous peoples. Information: (505) 989-8898

OCTOBER

Fall Festival of the Arts: Runs for 10 days. Features the work of painters, sculptors, ceramicists, and woodworkers. Information: (505) 988-3924, or write 1524 Paseo de Peralta, Santa Fe, NM 87501

NOVEMBER

Arts and Crafts Fair: Features folk dolls, fabric crafts, Spanish Colonial woodwork, wooden toys, and jewelry. Information: (505) 471-7873

PUEBLO DANCES AND FEAST DAYS

JANUARY

Various dances. *Most Pueblos.*

Transfer of Canes. *Most Pueblos, January 1.*

King's Day Celebration in honor of new Tribal Officers. Eagle, Elk, Buffalo, and Deer dances common. *Most Pueblos, January 6.*

San Ildefonso Feast Day. Begins with vespers the evening before, followed by a procession around the Plaza and dancing by the Game Priest, Buffalo, Buffalo Woman, and Deer. The next day, these dancers appear again at dawn; a mass, another procession, and more dancing follow. *San Ildefonso, January 23.*

FEBRUARY

Candelaria Day, with Buffalo and other dances. *Picuris, Santo Domingo, and San Felipe, February 2.*

Hopi Bean dance. *Date variable.*

Buffalo, Deer, and Animal dances. *San Juan and Santa Clara, date variable.*

MARCH

San José Feast Day, with the Harvest dance. *Laguna, March 19.*

APRIL

Various dances. *Most Pueblos, Easter week.*

MAY

San Felipe Feast Day. Includes an early morning mass, followed by a procession bearing an image of the Saint. Feasts complete the day. *San Felipe, May 1.*

Santa Cruz Day, with the Corn dance. *Taos and Cochiti, May 3.*

Corn dance. *Tesuque, late May to early June.*

JUNE

San Antonio Feast Day, with the Corn dance. *Sandia, San Ildefonso, San Juan, Santa Clara, and Taos, June 13.*

San Juan Feast Day, with Buffalo dance, begins at vespers the evening before. *San Juan, June 24.*

Corn dance *(Taos)* and Grab Day *(Cochiti), June 24.*

San Pedro Feast Day, with Corn dances. *San Felipe, Santa Ana, and Santo Domingo, June 29.*

JULY

High Country Arts & Crafts Festival. *Picuris, first weekend.*

Nambe Falls Celebration. *Nambe, July 4.*

Taos Pueblo Pow-Wow. *Taos, July 7 to 9.*

Española Fiesta with parades, historical pageantry, and food. *Picuris, second weekend.*

San Buenaventura Feast Day, with early mass, the Corn dance, and ritual clowns. *Cochiti, July 14.*

Fiesta de Santiago, with mass, food, and entertainment. *Chimayó, third weekend.*

Annual Northern Pueblo Artist and Craftsman Show. *San Ildefonso, July 21 to 22.*

Santiago Feast Day, featuring Grab Day, where people sharing Saint's name throw food from their roofs. *San Felipe, Acoma, Cochiti, Laguna, Santo Domingo, San Ildefonso, and Taos, July 25.*

Santa Ana Feast Day, with mass, processions, the Corn dance, and Horse dancers. *Santa Ana, July 26.*

Puye Cliffs Ceremonial, with dances by Santa Clara, Nambe, and San Ildefonso Pueblos at their ancestral ruins. *Puye Cliffs, last weekend.*

AUGUST

Old Pecos Bull Dance, in celebration of Nuestra Señora de los Angeles, patron of the extinct Pecos Pueblo whose survivors live at Jemez. *Jemez, August 2.*

Pueblo Plaza Fiesta. *Pojoaque, August 4.*

Santo Domingo Feast Day, with an early mass and procession, ritual clowns, the largest Corn dance with 500 dancers, and procession at sunset back to the church. *Santo Domingo, August 4.*

San Lorenzo Feast Day. Celebrations begin in Picuris with Sunset dance the evening before; the next day features a ceremonial relay race, dancing and a pole-climb to retrieve a sheep carcass. Penasco has a carnival, Acoma a Corn dance, and Laguna and Cochiti have Grab Day. *August 10.*

Santa Clara Feast Day, with Corn, Harvest, and Buffalo or Comanche dances after mass. *Santa Clara, August 12.*

Feast Day to honor Nuestra Señora de las Asunción, with mass, processions, ritual clowns, and the Corn dance. *Zia, August 15.*

Spanish Fiesta to honor San Augustin, with a carnival and mass but no dancing. *Isleta, August 28.*

Corn dances. *San Ildefonso, late August through early September.*

SEPTEMBER

San Estevan Feast Day. The Acoma people return to the old mesa-top Pueblo for a fiesta with mass in the magnificent mission church, processions, and dancing. *Acoma, September 2.*

Continuation of San Augustin's Feast Day at Isleta. Carnival, Spanish and Indian music and dancing, and a bonfire the evening before; an early mass and procession, a feast, and the Harvest dance follow on the next day. *Isleta, September 4.*

Celebration of La Natividad de la Virgen, with the Harvest and social dances at Laguna, and a Corn dance at San Ildefonso. *September 8.*

Fiesta de Santa Fe, the most elaborate of the Spanish fiestas, celebrates the Spanish reconquest of the city in 1692. Friday evening the 40-foot-tall puppet Zozobra is burned, and the weekend continues with many other activities. *Santa Fe, weekend after Labor Day.*

San Geronimo Feast Day begins the evening before with vespers, a sundown dance, and drumming and singing that last through the night. *Taos, September 30.*

San Francisco Feast Day, with vespers and a firelight procession the evening before and various dances on the feast day itself. *Nambe, October 4.*

NOVEMBER

San Diego Feast Day. In Jemez there is a mass, the Corn dance, clowns, and a trade fair. Tesuque's festival includes a Deer dance at dawn, mass, and a procession. *Jemez and Tesuque, November 12.*

DECEMBER

Shalako Ceremony, which lasts for 24 hours. Nine-foot-tall Shalako figures dance in newly built or remodeled houses to bless them. At dawn the Shalakos engage in a ritual race on stilts. *Zuni, early December.*

Feast Day in honor of Nuestra Señora de Guadalupe. After mass there are Bow and Arrow, Buffalo, or Comanche dances. In Jemez the dance called Los Matachines is performed, which portrays the struggle between good and evil. In Nambe, the Deer dance is performed. *Jemez, Nambe, and Pojoaque, December 12.*

Sundown torchlight procession honoring La Virgen. Ceremony also includes vespers and Los Matachines. *Taos, Picuris, and San Juan, December 24.*

Los Matachines and various other dances. *Taos, Tesuque, San Ildefonso, Santa Clara, and Picuris, December 25.*

Turtle Dance. *San Juan, December 26.*

Los Santos Inocentes Ceremony, children's dances. *Santa Clara, December 28.*

IMPORTANT TELEPHONE NUMBERS

(505 area code for all numbers)

Eight Northern Indian Pueblos Council
852-4265

Nambe Pueblo
455-2036

Picuris Pueblo
587-2957

Pojoaque Pueblo
455-2278

San Ildefonso Pueblo
455-2273

San Juan Pueblo
852-4400

Santa Clara Pueblo
753-7326

Taos Pueblo
758-9593

Tesuque Pueblo
983-2667

Santa Fe Convention and Visitors' Bureau
984-6760, (800) 528-5369

Santa Fe Chamber of Commerce
983-7317

Los Alamos Chamber of Commerce
662-8105

Espanola Chamber of Commerce
753-2831

Taos County Chamber of Commerce
758-3873

New Mexico Economic Development and Tourism Department
827-0300, (800) 545-2040

New Mexico State Park and Recreation Division
827-7465